Cornerstones of Freedom

The Story of

THE UNITED NATIONS

By R. Conrad Stein

Illustrated by Ralph Canaday

CHILDRENS PRESS ®

CHICAGO

Library of Congress Cataloging-in-Publication Data

Stein, R. Conrad.
  The story of the United Nations.

  (Cornerstones of freedom)
  Includes index.
  Summary: Describes the history, organization, and
functions of the United Nations.
    1.   United Nations—Juvenile literature.
[1.   United Nations]   I.   Title.   II.   Series.
JX1977.Z8S79   1986   341.23   85-31356
ISBN 0-516-04698-5

In the fall of 1962 President John F. Kennedy
received a report that the Russians were installing
medium-range ballistic missiles in Cuba. To
investigate the claim, the president ordered United
States reconnaissance planes on a secret photogra-
phy mission. The planes came back with remarkably
clear pictures. Now there were no doubts. The
Soviet Union, trying to gain a quick advantage over
the United States in the delicate balance of power,
was placing offensive missiles in Cuba, just ninety
miles from U.S. soil.

On October 22, 1962, President Kennedy gave a
chilling speech over national television that those
watching will never forget. He made public an order

he had issued to the U.S. Navy to "quarantine" all Soviet ships heading toward Cuba. This meant American warships would stop Soviet freighters, board them, and search them for missiles before allowing the ships to proceed. If the Russian ships refused to stop, they would be fired on and possibly sunk. The American president had issued a deadly challenge to the Russians. The two nations were inches away from a devastating nuclear war.

The next day the drama of the Cuban Missile Crisis shifted to the United Nations building in New York City. Speaking before the Security Council, the U.S. ambassador, Adlai Stevenson, demanded that the Russians remove their missiles from Cuba at once. Soviet Ambassador Valerian Zorin at first

GREAT BRITAIN

UNITED STATES

implied that there were no Russian missiles on the island. Stevenson, growing angry, said, "Do you, Ambassador Zorin, deny that the USSR has placed and is placing medium- and intermediate-range missiles and sites in Cuba? Yes or no?"

The Soviet ambassador listened through earphones while a United Nations translator related Stevenson's question in the Russian language. But Stevenson believed Zorin had understood his question, and he shouted out, "Don't wait for the translation. Yes or no?"

Finally Zorin said he would answer the question "in due course."

"I am prepared to wait for my answer until hell freezes over," Stevenson replied.

As the debate raged on the floor of the United Nations, U Thant, the secretary-general of the organization, quietly offered compromise proposals to the two feuding nations. Finally, after endless hours of tense negotiations, it was agreed that the Soviet Union would remove its missiles, and the Cubans would allow a UN inspection team to visit the island to make sure the missiles were gone.

The Cuban Missile Crisis was over. With help from the United Nations the world had been spared a war that could have been destructive enough to alter life on this planet. The United Nations' role as a peacemaker during the crisis was a fulfillment of its founders' dreams.

The United Nations was born during a war in the hope of preventing future wars. Late in World War II, the Allied powers sought to create an organization to keep the peace after the war ended. The Allies dreamed of forming a large assembly of nations that would provide peaceful methods of settling disputes.

The idea for a worldwide alliance for peace was not new. At the end of World War I an organization called the League of Nations was established. The League of Nations had the same major goal as the present-day United Nations. The member nations hoped to resolve international problems in a peaceful manner. One of the most enthusiastic supporters of the League of Nations was American President Woodrow Wilson. But, in the United States, all treaties must be ratified by the Senate. The American Senate refused to let the president sign the treaty that would make the United States a

member of the League of Nations. The overriding
reason for the Senate's action was a feeling of isola-
tionism that swept the country after World War I. It
was generally believed that the United States
should separate, or isolate itself, from problems aris-
ing elsewhere in the world.

The League of Nations lasted a little more than
twenty years. It was for the most part an ineffective
body. Before World War II a number of skirmishes

broke out that the League was unable to stop. In 1935 Italy invaded Ethiopia. Later a bloody civil war erupted in Spain. Finally Germany attacked Poland, the League of Nations collapsed, and the world plunged into the most costly war in history.

The League of Nations failed as a peacekeeping body primarily because the United States was not a member. America had become the most powerful country of the twentieth century, and its absence doomed the old League of Nations from its start. But the lessons of World War II were too important to ignore. The war had left millions dead and destroyed entire cities. Sensible people in the U.S. and elsewhere began to demand that a strong peacekeeping alliance of nations be established.

On August 21, 1944, while the war still raged, representatives of the United States, the Soviet Union, Great Britain, and China met in a handsome old estate near Washington, D.C., called Dumbarton Oaks. Delegates to this Dumbarton Oaks Conference agreed to establish a new organization to be called the United Nations (UN). On April 25, 1945, again while World War II still was being fought, men and women of forty-six nations gathered at San Francisco to draft a charter for the new UN.

If any of the delegates still doubted the need for a worldwide peacekeeping body, their doubts vanished on August 6, 1945. On that day a single American bomber dropped a single atomic bomb, obliterating the Japanese city of Hiroshima. Clearly this terrible new weapon could destroy all life on earth. The United Nations was not only desirable, it was now vital.

On October 24, 1945, the new United Nations was born. Today we hail that date as UN Day. In the United States the old isolationist feelings had disappeared entirely. This time the American Senate chose to join the organization by the overwhelming vote of 89 to 2.

The founders of the United Nations drew up a charter to state the purposes and functions of the

organization. The charter is similar to a country's
constitution. The original charter listed four major
aims the UN hoped to achieve: (1) to keep the peace,
(2) to encourage nations to be just in their dealings
with each other, (3) to promote cooperation between
countries, and (4) to provide an agency where all
nations can work together in harmony.

Certainly keeping the peace is the most important goal of the UN. The first sentence of the charter reads, "We, the peoples of the United Nations, determined to save succeeding generations from the scourge of war which twice in our lifetime has brought untold sorrow to mankind. . . ." The UN's peacekeeping operations fall primarily on three separate bodies: the Security Council, the General Assembly, and the office of the secretary-general.

When the charter was written, the Security Council was looked upon as the UN's major peacekeeping agency. Dominated by the large powers, it was to act as an international "police force" and send troops to restore peace in any of the world's trouble spots. It was hoped that the five major nations that won World War II—the United States, the Soviet Union, Great Britain, France, and China—would continue to work together on the Security Council.

But disagreements quickly developed among these great powers. Three years after the birth of the UN, a Communist revolution succeeded in China and the old Chinese government was forced to flee to the island of Taiwan. The United States wanted the deposed government to retain its seat on the

Security Council, even though it now represented only a tiny minority of the Chinese people. The Russians demanded that the new Communist government replace the old one. The U.S. and its allies won the initial dispute, and it was not until 1971 that Communist China was allowed to take a permanent seat on the Security Council. The squabble over the China question, however, weakened the effectiveness of the Security Council.

The Security Council is made up of fifteen member nations, five of which are called "permanent."

The five permanent members are the United States, Russia, China, Great Britain, and France. Also ten "temporary" members are elected for two-year terms by the UN as a whole. The rules state that any of the five permanent members can vote against, or veto, any action of the Security Council. For example, in 1950 Communist forces from North Korea invaded South Korea. The Security Council voted to send troops to repel the invasion. Russia certainly would have vetoed that action. But at the time the Russian delegation was boycotting the UN in protest over the Security Council's refusal to seat Communist China. Over the years Russia has exercised its veto in the Security Council more than one hundred times.

Because of struggles among the great powers, the Security Council has lost much of its ability to keep the peace. In recent years the UN's peacekeeping role has fallen more and more on the General Assembly and the office of the secretary-general.

The General Assembly is a worldwide congress. It is the only body in the UN in which every nation has one vote. No single nation is able to veto an act of the General Assembly. Its powers as a peacekeeping body were greatly enhanced in 1950 when it passed the "Uniting for Peace" resolution. This resolution gave the General Assembly the authority to act on a dangerous situation when the Security Council was rendered powerless by vetoes.

An important function of the General Assembly is to provide a worldwide forum for nations that are either at war or on the brink of war. This kind of public debate was helpful in finding a peaceful solution during the dangerous Cuban Missile Crisis. Today important sessions of the General Assembly can be carried via satellite to almost every television

Trusteeship Council		Security Council

General Assembly

International Court of Justice		Secretariat

Economic and Social Council

set in the world. Sometimes angry delegates exchange insults and curses on the floor of the General Assembly. Once Soviet Premier Nikita Khrushchev took off his shoe and pounded it on the table to drive home a point during a General Assembly debate. But fiery words and gestures are always preferable to bombs and missiles.

The secretary-general is the chief administrator of the UN and could be thought of as its chairman or mayor. The secretary-general is nominated by the Security Council and is approved by a majority vote of the General Assembly. He or she serves a five-year term and can be reelected.

All five permanent members of the Security Council must agree on a candidate for the office before the name goes to the General Assembly for the final vote. To satisfy all the great powers, a person from one of the nonaligned countries (those that are neither Communist nor non-Communist) is usually chosen.

The secretary-general is vital to the UN's peacekeeping functions. The charter authorizes him to advise the Security Council on any war-threatening situation. He has a similar role with the General Assembly. Also he acts as a mediator in disputes between all powers, large or small. Secretary-General U Thant helped mediate the Cuban Missile Crisis because his integrity had won the confidence of both the Soviets and the Americans. The secretary-general is more flexible in mediating disputes than is a large body such as the General Assembly or a divided body such as the Security Council.

Men of extraordinary ability have occupied the secretary-general's office. The Norwegian Trygve Lie, elected in 1946, was the UN's first secretary-general. One of the most revered secretaries-general was the Swede Dag Hammarskjöld, who served from 1953 to 1961. He helped ease tensions between the United States and the Soviet Union. Hammarskjöld died in a 1961 plane crash while on a UN mission to Africa. U Thant, a Burmese diplomat, served from 1961 to 1972 while many African and Asian countries were in chaos. Kurt Waldheim of Austria was secretary-general from 1972 to 1982. He helped resolve a dangerous war that flared up in the Middle East. Javier Pérez de Cuéllar of Peru succeeded Waldheim and became the UN's fifth secretary-general. All the men who have held the office were known for their intelligence, their energy, and above all, their fairness.

Another UN peacekeeping body is the International Court of Justice. Its fifteen judges are appointed by both the Security Council and the General Assembly. This court hears arguments from countries that are locked in a dispute and then makes a judgment. The dispute might be a disagreement over national boundaries or over fishing rights

Secretaries–General
of the United Nations

Trygve Lie
1946-1953

Dag Hammarskjöld
1953-1961

U Thant
1961-1972

Kurt Waldheim
1972-1982

Javier Pérez de Cuéllar
1982-

in the ocean. One weakness plaguing the court is that it has no way of enforcing its decisions. For example, in May 1980, the International Court of Justice ordered the revolutionary government of Iran to release the American hostages it captured during a raid on the U.S. embassy in Tehran. But the Iranian government ignored the order and held the people prisoner until January 1981.

The UN's peacekeeping efforts have met with both successes and failures. In its forty-year history it has never faced a conflict of the awesome magnitude of World War II. But the Vietnam War raged for years despite the UN's efforts to bring about a settlement. The UN was also powerless to prevent the 1982 Falkland Islands War between Argentina and Great Britain. On the other hand, the UN was able to arrange cease-fires in the complex and volatile Middle East when wars between Arabs and Israelis broke out there in 1967 and 1973.

Peacekeeping is the most obviously dramatic activity of the UN. But the organization's efforts to improve the welfare of the world's people have achieved equally dramatic results.

One goal stated in the UN charter is to "promote social progress and better standards of life." To help give the world a better standard of living, the UN has created agencies staffed by technicians from all over the world. These technicians might be doctors, teachers, or farming experts. They are sent to poor countries where they introduce modern methods of growing food, combating disease, and teaching people to read. UN agencies have achieved some stunning triumphs in social welfare.

At one time smallpox was the most deadly disease to affect mankind. Over its long and dark history, smallpox killed hundreds of millions of people and left many more permanently scarred and blinded. Vaccines were developed, and by the 1940s the disease had been eliminated in Europe and North America. But smallpox still scourged Africa, Asia, and South America. Then, in 1967, a UN agency called the World Health Organization (WHO) began a campaign to eradicate this ancient plague forever.

Health care workers from WHO trekked into the tiniest villages in the remotest corners of the world. They vaccinated people and isolated those already afflicted. Because of their massive efforts only six cases of smallpox were reported anywhere on earth in 1973. In 1980 WHO announced that the curse of smallpox no longer existed. It was the first time in history that an organized human crusade had eradicated a disease from this planet.

In the United States Halloween is a time for trick-or-treating. But millions of American children trick-or-treat for UNICEF, asking for donations instead of candy. UNICEF is the United Nations Children's Fund. It is an agency that provides food, medicine, and clothing for needy children. UNICEF was created by the General Assembly in 1946 to aid the millions of suffering children then living in war-torn lands. Its work was so popular that the UN made UNICEF a permanent agency in 1953. About one-fourth of its funds are donated by private parties such as American trick-or-treaters. The remainder of its money comes from UN member nations. In 1965 UNICEF won the Nobel Peace Prize for its work with children in more than one hundred nations.

The constitution of a UN agency called UNESCO starts with the words, "Since wars begin in the minds of men, it is in the minds of men that the defenses of peace must be constructed." UNESCO is the United Nations Educational, Scientific, and Cultural Organization. It was established in 1946, and the agency is headquartered in Paris, France. It encourages the work of artists, scientists, thinkers, and poets. One of its primary goals is to teach people in developing countries how to read. UNESCO trains teachers and provides books so that people

from families that have been illiterate for generations can experience the joy of reading.

In the 1970s the populations of underdeveloped countries soared while their food production declined. The result was mass starvation. The major UN agency devoted to fighting hunger is the Food and Agriculture Organization (FAO), established in 1945. Farm experts from the FAO teach modern agriculture to people who are hardworking farmers, but whose methods are outdated. Another UN agency called the World Food Council (established in

1974) distributes food to areas that are suffering from famine. Unfortunately, these two agencies were unable to offset the disastrous famine that gripped parts of Africa in the mid-1980s.

Today the glittering UN building in New York City is a favorite spot for groups of tourists and schoolchildren. The enormous meeting hall remains a unique assembly of nations. In the 1980s the UN has grown to more than 150 member nations, with new countries still being admitted. Many of the members are small, developing countries that once were colonies of European powers. Some critics complain that these states now control the UN with their votes, while large countries such as the United States are left to pay most of the bills.

But despite its detractors, most people realize that the United Nations is our only form of world government. It is our best hope to prevent war. President John F. Kennedy expressed this sentiment when he spoke before the General Assembly in 1961 and said, "Together we shall save our planet or together we shall perish in its flames. Save it we can, and save it we must, and then we shall earn the eternal thanks of mankind and, as peacemakers, the eternal blessing of God."

About the Author

R. Conrad Stein was born and grew up in Chicago. He enlisted in the Marine Corps at the age of eighteen and served for three years. He then attended the University of Illinois where he received a bachelor's degree in history. He later studied in Mexico, earning an advanced degree from the University of Guanajuato. Mr. Stein is the author of many other books, articles, and short stories written for young people.

Mr. Stein now lives in Chicago with his wife, Deborah Kent, who is also a writer of books for young readers, and their daughter Janna.

About the Artist

Ralph Canaday has been involved in all aspects of commercial art since graduation from the Art Institute of Chicago in 1959. He is an illustrator, designer, painter, and sculptor whose work has appeared in many national publications, textbooks, and corporate promotional material. Mr. Canaday lives in Hanover Park, Illinois, with his wife Arlene, who is also in publishing.